D1320476

InterVarsity Press
Downers Grove
Illinois 60515

How to begin an evangelistic Bible study

Ada Lum

Fourth printing, May 1974

InterVarsity Press is the book publishing division of Inter-Varsity Christian Fellowship, a student movement active on campus at hundreds of universities, colleges and schools of nursing. For information about this dynamic association, write IVCF, 233 Langdon, Madison, WI 53703. If you're a student, four chances out of five you'll find a local IVCF chapter on your campus.

ISBN 0-87784-317-1

Printed in the United States of America

CONTENTS

1 HOW CAN WE GET NON-CHRISTIANS INTERESTED IN STUDYING THE BIBLE WITH US?

As I write this I am stimulated in mind and spirit from a conversation yesterday with a young minister about our Christian outreach. As an overseas student in Australia he had been converted to Jesus Christ. Knowing that workshops on evangelistic Bible studies had been held on the nearby campus, he asked, "How can we get non-Christians interested in studying the Bible with us?"

We shared ideas. He told about the first time he began an evangelistic Bible study. He was living in a flat with several other overseas students. They apparently were "typical bachelors." Housekeeping—well, there wasn't any! Books, clothes, records were strewn all over. Dirty dishes were not piled up on the kitchen sink; they were left on the table or floor. Garbage was not removed.

Several times he thought of moving out, but he knew that God had a reason for putting him there, as the only Christian in the group. So he began to clean up the mess, wash the dishes and take out the garbage. He had opportunity to be the peacemaker in a violent quarrel between two who were brothers.

Then he noticed that for all their studies they still had free time. So one day he casually suggested, "Say, we don't seem to have much to do this afternoon. You all know I'm a Christian. How about a discussion on Christianity—like

Christianity and science?" Being an adventurous, if not fastidious, lot, they answered, "Sure, why not?"

That opening discussion led to a series of Bible studies in the now clean flat. Then the Christian, knowing his roommates needed a broader encounter with Christians, invited them to go with him to a nearby church. The pastor and the people were open and hospitable, and the corporate witness of the Christian community greatly reinforced the young Christian's witness. Eventually some were converted.

This story vividly illustrates one way to begin an evangelistic Bible study. Four things are necessary:

☐ The conviction that God has put us in certain environments to be his witnesses.

☐ Genuine friendship which involves God's "in-spite-of" kind of love. Such a love is willing to be a servant to others, *in spite of* their not deserving it.

☐ Sensitivity to judge the right time to invite others to a no-strings-attached discussion about Christianity. This discussion can then lead to solid Bible studies.

☐ Wisdom to know how to introduce an interested non-Christian to the larger fellowship of the body of Christ.

Think of how students trained in these principles of Bible study leadership and personal evangelism multiply the ranks of disciple-makers! In the Philippines IVCF staff members are available on weekends to assist local churches in training Bible study leaders. The goal of the National Fellowship for Philippine Evangelism is to establish 10,000 lay evangelistic Bible study groups by the end of 1973.

The principle is clear: Staff and graduates in the local churches must teach others to teach others to teach others to teach others . . . (2 Tim. 2:2).

2 WHAT IS AN EVANGELISTIC BIBLE STUDY ANYHOW?

The Evangelistic Bible Study (EBS) is not a new "method" of evangelism. But it is a neglected one. It is at least as old as the first century when Philip "went ... heard ... asked ... [listened to the answer] ... then opened his mouth, and beginning with this scripture he told him the good news of Jesus" (Acts 8:26-40).

The EBS is different from Bible studies which are geared for Christians. The latter, "pastoral" Bible studies, aim for mutual upbuilding. The EBS is for non-Christians, since Christians presumably do not need to be evangelized. It may consist of only two people—the Christian and his friend—or six to eight people, depending on the circumstances. In any case it should never be dominated by Christians.

The EBS is demanding because it requires our best all-around efforts as "beggars." (D. T. Niles has defined a Christian witness as "one beggar telling another beggar where to find food.") It requires that we regard the inquiring non-believer as a whole person, not merely as a "soul." He or she is a person with intelligence, feelings and integrity of individual will. The EBS requires that we "give ourselves away" as fellow human beings, just as Paul did to the Thessalonians (1 Thess. 2:8).

The EBS is a contrast and a complement to other evangelistic methods. Much of our evangelism is *extensive*—large lecture meetings, special missions, musical programs, etc. Or, it is communicating the gospel directly or indirectly during *brief encounters* with strangers, as in sharing our faith with a seat companion on the train, giving out tracts, knocking on doors and other short-lived contacts.

But most of us normally live in a settled community. Here we have the responsibility of *intensive* evangelism, that is, concentrating on one or two or three seekers in a *sustained* way. Here nothing is more effective than the *personal* evangelistic Bible study fellowship. Here we can invite our friends who show confusion, vagueness or a fragmented knowledge of the gospel. Here none of us will feel rushed or pressured but can calmly examine the facts about Jesus Christ.

Definition: The Evangelistic Bible Study is a study/discussion on selected gospel passages which vitally confront the participants with the person of Jesus Christ, not merely with facts about Christianity. The aim is to stimulate non-Christians to consider seriously the fact that Jesus Christ is the God-man who deserves our ultimate love and loyalty.

The EBS is best held in an informal but regular, quiet place that is natural to your friends. The number of times it is held is flexible; people and circumstances vary. It may last for a few weeks, one or two times, or a year. Play it by ear.

When inviting the cautious inquirer perhaps all we can appeal to initially is, "Would you like to take an hour this Saturday evening to see what the Bible really says about Jesus?" Some are ripe and ready to commit themselves to a series of six to eight studies. Others will respond to, "Some of us are going to be studying a very helpful guide to basic Christianity. Would you like to join us? It's only four studies long." Later, if their interest is captured, the studies can be extended.

In general, students like to keep such a study open-ended. Keep in mind that you need about six to eight weeks to cover the basics of Christianity. Begin early in the school year after you have had time to develop real friend-ships with non-Christians. End the studies before examination jitters crop up.

3 SKIP THIS SECTION IF YOU'RE ALREADY CONVINCED THAT THE EBS IS RESPONSIBLE EVANGELISM

The Bible is worth studying. Non-Christians may unthinkingly criticize or disagree with it. But no one can contradict that it has been the world's greatest literary influence and still remains the world's best seller. When we invite others to study the Bible with us, we do not require that they accept it as God's Word. We need only agree that it is worth studying!

Consider the realism and wisdom of the Evangelistic Bible Study approach throughout the campus.

1/It takes the university scene seriously.

In Asia, as elsewhere, there is an increasing restlessness with the authoritarian method of teaching, the unquestioning acceptance of the lecturer's content. Students are being trained in the investigative approach to learning, that is, examining the facts, seeing the implications, and then drawing conclusions. Today there is a growing desire among students for questioning and dialogue. Campus issues no longer have neat, packaged answers—if they ever did. Neither does Christianity.

2/It takes the individual seriously.

The EBS respects the intelligence and integrity of the individual to examine for himself the life and the claims of Jesus Christ. This is not the same as catering to intellectual arrogance. Most university students are not truly intellectual. But they are intelligent! So the EBS requires not that the Christian be intellectual about Christianity, but intelligent about the text being studied and the reasons for his beliefs. The *tone* of the EBS is characterized by the question, "What makes sense to both of us?"

3/It provides small-group at-easeness.
All of us need this, especially freshmen coming into a new campus and new social life. People are more at ease discussing religious subjects in an informal, friendly atmosphere of just a few people. And this we have lately discovered: The very atmosphere of openness and honesty that the EBS encourages begins to tell the non-Christian what genuine Christian fellowship is like.

4/It does not depend on staff or professionally trained men for leadership.
Students can be and have been trained to lead an EBS even more effectively than some staff! A letter from a Filipino student demonstrates the truth of this principle: "Since our workshops on leading Bible studies, we have had our own members lead, no longer having to depend so much on the pastors and missionaries. The leaders are often thrilled at the work of the Holy Spirit and to discover their talents as Bible study leaders."

5/It is responsible personal evangelism.
It is a realistic and sustained effort in reaching others for Christ. It clarifies the good news in a situation where all parties involved are interacting honestly as persons, and not merely as the hunter and the hunted in an artificial "game preserve."

When a Christian gives himself to the Lord to be disciplined and stimulated by commitment to the EBS, he will make new discoveries about God and about himself. He will grow as a person. And he will come to understand and love non-Christians more. It's inevitable!

4 WALK AROUND IN HIS SKIN FOR A WHILE (WHY WE DON'T GET ACROSS)

At a GKM (Inter-Varsity Christian Fellowship in Thailand) conference on campus evangelism I was among a group of Asian students and staff who went out each afternoon to apply what we had learned in the morning. Natural anxiety turned to sheer joy to see how God opened ears and hearts. We discovered that every one of us, including the Thais themselves, had wrong preconceptions about the Buddhists, for example, that Buddhists don't believe in God.

Being the least Thai, I especially had to rid myself not only of stereotyped ideas about Buddhists, but also of preconceptions of the modern, educated Thai Buddhist. In fact it was not until I had talked with many of them and reflected on our conversations that I could even begin to get across to their island of interests and heart concerns. I had to try to walk around in their Thai Buddhist skin for a while. I was not very successful but it helped!

Stereotypes, preconceptions and hasty conclusions about each other (on the part of both Christians and non-Christians) raise barriers to effective communication.

There are still other reasons why we do not get across. One, possibly a Western difficulty, is the insistence that we always approach truth logically. We tend to think that if we only present the facts of the gospel in a logical order, surely people should respond.

Second, there is an evangelical conditioning that makes

us overly intent on orthodox theology and precise wording of biblical belief and experience—as we have been trained in it.

Finally, we have defensive preconceptions of what non-Christians are like—we are sure they are all hard and argumentative.

So we keep giving answers to unasked questions. Or we feel a rush of correction fluid coursing through our veins when even a minor theological cloudiness appears. Or we overexplain. Or we become defensive in a "we-they" mentality when our ego-involved views are challenged.

Walk around in his skin for a while. What are his anxieties as he tries to rearrange his inherited religious ideas in a changing society that fascinates him? How is his social pattern changing in the big city? What are the pressures he endures as the first member of his family to receive a university education? What does he think about love and marriage now that he knows his parents probably will not arrange for his wife? How are his ideas about "the Western religion" different from his parents' since he has been exposed to much Western literature with biblical presuppositions?

In the United States the non-Christian is up against other pressure. What does he do with the tension created when his parents push him toward a middle-class, materialistic life-style and his peers pull him toward a "return-to-nature"? How does he react to the existing political system? Does he ignore it? Quietly work from within to change the structure? Or break out and adopt revolutionary principles and tactics? What does he think about the increasing sexual freedom and the accelerating trend toward "conditional" or "temporary" marriages or whatever? How does he cope with cultural despair—the message of most of the popular arts?

Our self-image may be a barrier to a clear witness. I once

asked a group of students to write briefly what they thought their peers' concepts of Jesus Christ and Christians were. Frankly, I was primarily interested to know what the Christian self-image was. About three-fourths of the papers indicated a very negative concept of themselves. The Christians in that university had an inferiority complex! No wonder a ghetto climate was growing.

A Christian ghetto is contradictory to Christ's great commission (Mt. 28:18-20). But we can begin to "go and make disciples" only by understanding other people and opening our lives to them. By the way—this is love.

5 HOW CAN WE GET THE GOOD NEWS ACROSS?

When we are preparing the Bible study and praying for our non-Christian friends, we should ask God to give us a fresh understanding of how they really think and feel, and how their reacting apparatus works. Keep in mind that for them to consider Jesus Christ seriously the EBS must be relevant, personal, powerful and thought-provoking.

1/*The EBS must be relevant.*

Once I was in an EBS when we considered Luke 5:12-16 on Jesus' cleansing a leper. A Hindu student curiously asked why Jesus was not afraid of contracting the ugly disease when he touched the man. A Christian nurse triumphantly answered, "Because he was the Son of God." Thud. The questioner said nothing. I wanted to shout, "Jesus took a risk! He took the human risk of becoming a leper for love's sake. That's why!"

While I debated exposing myself as possibly a heretical humanist, a Muslim interjected, "I would never touch a leper. I wouldn't think of going near one." We could have lost that strategic moment for explaining the really good news of Jesus. Fortunately, one of the other Christians casually commented, "I don't think Jesus was concerned about getting leprosy. He was concerned about helping the man." The non-Christians thereupon became visibly interested in what kind of person Jesus was after all. (So did the nurse.)

The purpose of the EBS is not to present the complete case for biblical Christianity each time. It is a bit more limited. The ultimate aim is that our friend may become an active disciple of Jesus Christ, our Lord. But the *immediate objective* in a given study is that he may respond positively to Christ, as did the Hindu and Muslim students in that Bible study. Surely such a response is just as much the creative, dynamic work of the Holy Spirit as is rebirth.

The question we face is, How can we *initially* capture modern man's attention to Jesus Christ? Well, how did God capture first-century man's attention? By human terms that human beings could understand. That is what the incarnation is all about. It is a fantastic fact of history that God became one of us. There is mystery here, and in the final analysis we cannot neatly divide the human nature of Christ from his divine nature.

But we must first grasp the New Testament facts of Jesus' humanity before we can approach the awesomeness and majesty of his deity. Even a cursory reading of the gospels reveals this was the order of experience for Jesus' disciples. The incarnation was not merely progressive understanding of God. The perfect humanity of Jesus reestablished God's orginal purpose for man, that he should have control over his whole environment (Heb. 2:5-18).

We study Jesus Christ so we can see what we should have been and can still become. Jesus Christ comes to us today as a Living Person, not as a Super Orthodox Idea.

In summary, the EBS (or any other Bible study) must be existentially relevant. It must aim to make Jesus Christ as Lord a live option for modern man. It must reveal what we are becoming as well as what we are and should be. It must help us to affirm our authentic humanity, not a sub-biblical humanity. And it must confront us with choices to be made now in the presence of the Redeemer-Christ, our Creator.

2/*The EBS must be personal and powerful.*

Paul the Apostle said of his three-week preaching mission which laid the foundation for the Thessalonian church:

For our gospel came to you not only in word, but also in power and in the Holy Spirit and with full conviction. You know what kind of men we proved to be among you, like a nurse taking care of her children. So, being affectionately desirous of you, we were ready to share with you not only the gospel of God but also our own selves, because you had become very dear to us. (1 Thess. 1:5; 2:7-8)

The clear implication here is that we cannot share the person of Jesus Christ and his gospel unless we are ready to share ourselves as persons—authentically—regarding others also as persons, and not as mere objects of our evangelistic efforts.

In the EBS Christians are essentially witnesses. Sometimes we fill a teaching role when we guide the study and explain certain points. But we do not seek to impress with superior Bible knowledge, experience or status. Indeed, it is a relief not to have to pretend to be mini-popes. We are still in the discipling process ourselves. But we are authoritative witnesses, authorized by the Divine Provider to invite fellow beggars to feast with us at his table.

Genuine enthusiasm for Jesus is contagious. There can be no phoniness here. Think of the Samaritan woman after she became convinced that Jesus spoke the truth. She *immediately* invited her townspeople (the very ones who had ostracized her) to investigate for themselves. "Many Samaritans from that city believed in him because of the woman's testimony" (Jn. 4:39).

The seeker will not ultimately be convinced by our witness, no matter how sincere we are in our approach. We are only pointers to God. But even though we are only human pointers, we must pray that we will point clearly. The Holy Spirit is the Divine Persuader. Jesus himself made this clear in John 14:26; 16:8, 13-15. Thank God! And so, as a practical friend often reminds me, "Prepare and work as though it all depended on you, but pray as though it all depended on God."

I do not fully understand what "power" means in 1 Thessalonians 1:5 as mentioned above. But it seems that it is the same power that Paul is thinking about in Romans 1:16, "[The gospel] is the power of God for salvation to every one who has faith." There is a force inherent in the gospel, apart from our best logical arguments, that moves men and women to respond to Christ.

If some of us do not truly believe this, we will be depending on eloquence, neat logic, personality, threats of hell, rewards of heaven and Madison Avenue to try to convince the unbeliever. If we are not convinced of God's power in his gospel, we must stop now and pray for faith.

3/The EBS must be thought-provoking.

Here are some practical guidelines in preparing a thought-provoking EBS.

First, We should select passages from the gospels. These are the historical records of the life and mission of Christ. (The epistles generally explain the implications of faith in Christ.) In the gospels we see Jesus in action; we are exposed to his unique life. Most non-Christians have vague ideas about Jesus because they simply do not know the facts in the gospel records. We must have an honest textual study in order to proceed to personal application based on concrete information.

Second, we must seek to understand the human situation described in the passage. Aim for an "on-the-spot reporter" description of the event. After all, your friend does not have the mental images of biblical scenes you already have. This is why subjective questions are sometimes asked at the beginning of a study. For example, What do you see, hear and smell in the temple courtyard? Or, more objectively,

Does anyone happen to know what the political situation of the Jewish nation was in the first century? Learn to guide the discussion so that the group can see that what happened in Jesus' time is realistically parallel to our decade.

Third, the discussion questions should lead the group to identify with the characters. The discussion questions should help us identify with the quietly desperate person who turns to Jesus for help, the know-it-all disciples, the compassionate Jesus himself, those who opposed him, and those who liked but did not understand him. Identification with the people in the story gives aliveness and warmth to the study. It helps us to interact with Jesus and thus leads more naturally to the consideration of his loving and powerful claim on us today.

So we might ask: What emotional conflicts must Nicodemus have felt at this point? Why do you suppose Simon Peter felt he knew better than Jesus what to do? What things did Jesus see in the people that stirred his compassion? How do you think the Pharisee was feeling when he said that to Jesus?

Fourth, Jesus must always be communicated as he was (and is)—warm, perceptive, totally responsive, accepting, controlled, controlling, capturing men's imaginations in a restless way until they became rightly related to him. Such a person always attracts the seeking non-believer, especially in our age of depersonalization and not-so-quiet desperation.

Fifth, Jesus' death and resurrection must be understood as central in our message. Jesus, very early in his own ministry (John 2:19), began to allude to this centrality. The apostolic preaching focused on the meaning of the crucifixion and the evidences of the resurrection. Obviously this does not mean we force the subject into every EBS; Jesus himself did not talk about it all the time. But it does mean that as the series of studies progresses, we move in the direction of examining the gospel records of Jesus' death and resurrection. We must also be ready at any time to discuss these subjects from the Bible when our friends ask why we emphasize them in our faith.

The gospels describe the details of Jesus' death on the cross, but for its significance we must study passages like Isaiah 53, Romans 5:6-11, 2 Corinthians 5:14-21 and 1 Peter 2:21-25.

6 MAYBE MY PROBLEM IS THAT I'M NOT EXCITED ABOUT JESUS CHRIST

That is exactly what a first-term missionary said to me. He was frankly responding to my comment that I did not see how we could even sound convincing in our witness if we were not enthusiastic about Jesus.

I did not mean we had to be bubbly and ready to dance a jig whenever we mention the name of Jesus. I meant that the healthy Christian, "who is giving all he knows of himself to all that he knows of Jesus Christ," is *alive* in his witness. He is happily convinced that Christ is the high, rightful Lord and Savior.

I really think my missionary friend basically loves Jesus Christ. Perhaps what he needs is to see Christ in a fresh, dynamic way. All of us can easily slip away from our first, bridal love for our Lord to sterile patterns of devotion.

Take the opportunity each time you prepare a study to watch Jesus in action as he interacted with people in the New Testament. Reflect . . . and reflect with fresh wonder and openness of heart.

The following questions on the facts, implications and significance of the life of Jesus can help bring out the emphasis of his uniqueness and his authority as the God-man.

☐ In what specific ways does Jesus show his interest in people as individuals? his understanding of their basic human needs and not just outward ones? What does he see in people and their human dilemmas that others apparently do not see? In what ways do his attitudes to people and their predicaments contrast with those of his contemporaries?

☐ What do you learn about human nature from Jesus' viewpoint? What does he command? What does he condemn?

☐ What happens when Jesus takes on the problems of his society—corruption, pride, ignorance, evil, cruelty, sickness, materialism? What traditions and prejudices does he come up against in doing so?

☐ How does Jesus affect people? Why? How do they affect him? Why? How does he bring out the best in people? How does he affirm their personal worth?

☐ What "human interest" details do you observe? What unique aspects of Jesus' personality and character does this event reveal? What fresh insights into his life mission do you now have?

☐ What are the implications of Jesus' life and Word for us today? What practical thing can you do this week to employ the truth you have learned?

Do not use the questions as they are. They are only broad guidelines for your personal study. They need specific rewording for your particular group. For example, if you are studying John 3:1-15 which records Jesus' conversation with the religious aristocrat Nicodemus, you will not want to ask, "How does Jesus show his interest in individuals?" Instead, use a sequence of questions which will precipitate insights: "What did Jesus already know about Nicodemus?" (Note: This is a factual question based on v. 10.) "Look at Jesus' response to Nicodemus' opening statement in v. 2. What hidden question did Jesus apparently see behind it?" (A question of implication.) "How do you think he really saw Nicodemus—only as a Pharisee, a ruler of the Jews?"

(Another question of implication.) "If Jesus could understand Nicodemus so well, what do you suppose he under-
stands about men today—you, for example?" (A question
of significance or application.)

7 A FEW SUGGESTIONS FOR LEADING STUDY DISCUSSIONS

Our basic responsibility as study leaders is *to guide the group into discovering what the Bible says and means.* We leave preaching to our ministers and keep our studies a true dialogue of give-and-take. For although we have leadership roles we are also learners. Here are some practical helps for encouraging others in the group to participate.

☐ Relax. Keep your sense of humor; be ready to laugh at yourself, too.

☐ Be enthusiastic without being irreverent or overpowering. Lead in such a way as to encourage honesty and confidence.

☐ Be ready with questions that will stimulate discussion and not simply require one-word answers.

☐ Resist the temptation to answer your own questions. Allow people time to think!

☐ Encourage questions from others, but refer them to the group.

☐ Keep the discussion moving by asking several people to contribute viewpoints, especially on strategic interpretation or application questions.

☐ Be sensitive to hesitant or shy members. Encourage them with a smile or a casual comment directed their way. Ask them questions that you are quite sure they can deal with, but which are not insultingly easy!

☐ It is not enough to listen to people. We must hear what

they are really saying. That is love. As a group member yourself, comment on their contributions or ask questions for clarification or elaboration, as you would in natural conversation.

☐ Allow freedom of expression so anyone in the group can say what is on his mind, but keep to the subject. Carefully challenge superficial answers by asking others to suggest additional ones.

☐ Let the Bible speak for itself. It is your authority. But this does not mean a non-Christian must accept it as God's Word before you can have honest discussion. Truth has its own quiet way of slipping into people.

☐ Summarize the discussion at the end of the study into one or two clear points of fresh knowledge, insight and challenge.

FOLLOWING THROUGH WITH PERSONAL CONVERSATIONS

End the study on time. Students are busy and not likely to be enthusiastic about returning if we habitually go over the agreed time. Besides, we can learn only one major point at a time—and this needs reflection.

It is more strategic to follow through with an individual in a more personal conversation after the study proper. We can always find an authentic conversational link based on the interaction we have already had in the study:

"I think you're still puzzled about what Jesus' view of sin is, aren't you? It's quite different from what a lot of people think today. . . ."

"What you said about Buddhist belief in earning merits was interesting. Did you know that God says it is impossible for man to earn his salvation?"

"I can see why you find it so difficult to believe that God loves us when you look only at the world's agony and people's problems. He feels deeply with us, and wants us, along with him, to be part of the solution. . . ."

In making this link you may find out more of what is on your friend's heart. Then you can proceed more directly to help him see his need (as a sinner) to confront the Lord Jesus and receive the gift of salvation.

The Holy Spirit will make you sensitive to the way he is leading in your friend's thinking. We need not pressure people to make decisions. We dare not! In God's timing and in

God's way that person will ask a crucial question or make a remark by which you will know that he is ready to welcome Christ into his life. And you will know it is not your human persuasion, but God's working.

When a friend does indicate a desire to commit himself to Jesus Christ and receive him as the Savior from his sin and the Lord of his life, show him that basically "there is something to believe and Someone to receive." Go over with him several basic steps that are involved in becoming a Christian:

☐ Believe that God loves you so much that he proved it by sending his only son Jesus into this crazy, mixed-up world to become your Savior (Jn. 3:16).

☐ Agree with Jesus that you must be born again if you want eternal (genuine) life and that this can be accomplished only by his Holy Spirit (Jn. 3:3).

☐ Repent of your self-willed, independent-from-God life (Acts 17:30, 2 Cor. 5:15).

☐ Accept Jesus' voluntary death on a criminal's cross as the payment for your sin and basis for your new life (1 Pet. 2:24).

☐ Welcome Jesus Christ into your life as your God, your Savior and your Friend. He is waiting to have fellowship with you (Rev. 3:20).

☐ Tell the Lord Jesus what you have just done. Do not worry about "proper" words. Simply talk to him as you would to a close friend whom you know loves and accepts you just as you are.

9 SUMMARY: EVALUATING AND IMPROVING THE EBS

This section is a summary-guide which you can use to check your effectiveness as an EBS leader. Most of the information has been covered in the previous sections. Certainly many of the points are plain common sense. But, as you anticipate leading an EBS, pray that the Holy Spirit will permeate your preparations, inspire your prayers for your friends and penetrate every contact you make for Jesus Christ.

About Your Friend
1/*He is an individual.* What things are important to him? What about his family? his problems? his ambitions? his frustrations? his religious background?
2/*He wants to be completely accepted as a person,* even if he comes in a bit drunk or stoned. He should feel free to be dressed any way he is comfortable. Christians, like their Lord who welcomed "sinners," should be unshockable— even by hippie smells.
3/*Where is he hurting?* What is his point of need? Identify with him there, but don't try to play clinical psychologist. It helps to remember that God is there with all his love and healing power.
4/*He doesn't want to be dominated by Christians.* Be sure that at least half of the participants in your study are non-Christians. Otherwise the EBS tends to be artificial; non-

Christians may get uncomfortable and react by becoming defensive or argumentative.

About the Climate
1/*Create an open, relaxed climate.* Emotions directly influence the process of learning. People tend to be anxious and uncomfortable when discussing religious subjects. Some may feel their cherished notions challenged and their security threatened. Guilt feelings complicate the situation more. Acceptance—love—helps to free them to consider new ideas.
2/*Sit in an informal circle,* so that all can look at each other comfortably. Be sure that everybody knows each other by full name. It is worth a few minutes at the start of each study to talk informally about mutual interests and concerns.
3/*It is better not to have any singing,* unless it is popular or folk songs which all know. Also praying before or after the study may be out of place. Consider what is fitting.
4/*A non-sectarian atmosphere encourages openness* when there are different churches represented. Our purpose is not to get people to change their churches, but to know Jesus Christ personally. The two issues must not be confused. For instance, if there is conflict in different denominational views, or between Roman Catholic and Protestant views, and the passage is not clear, summarize the alternatives as best you can, and move on.
5/*Avoid a comparative religions discussion,* especially when there are Muslims, Hindus, Buddhists or representatives of other religions present. It is generally better not to use the terms "Christianity" and "Christians," since these have formal connotations for most people. Instead use, "The Bible says" or "God says in the Bible" or "According to the record," when referring to the Christian faith. In a personal vein we can sometimes say, "I have come to see. . . ." Instead of "becoming a Christian," we might say "to become

a child of God" or "to begin the new life with Christ," etc.

6/*Honesty in personal testimony is essential.* Our witness is to Jesus Christ and his accomplishments, not to our problem-free lives. In speaking of the joys of knowing him, we must also show that he is Lord of the human problems which, realistically, we all have. Let's take off our masks. At times it will do wonders in the group for a Christian to say, "I don't know the answer to that problem, but I'll look into it and try to find an answer before we meet again."

7/*The Christian must have no sense of spiritual superiority.* The Christian is a sinner who knows God has forgiven and accepted him. The non-Christian is a sinner who does not know that yet. Martin Luther has challenged us to "Dare to be a sinner!" When we rightfully understand this challenge, we are gloriously liberated!

About the Study Itself

1/*To avoid confusion it is preferable to use only one version of the Bible.* This should be a modern translation so that those unfamiliar with the Bible can turn to a page and paragraph number rather than to a book, chapter and verse. You can obtain gospel portions at very low prices from the local Bible society, bookstore or IVCF campus booktable. Catholic editions of the RSV and the TEV can be obtained also.

2/*The study must be relevant to the non-Christian's needs and level of understanding.* How can you know what these are? "Listen" to what a person is saying to you non-verbally.

3/*The study must be contemporary.* A modern version of the Bible will help eliminate the idea that Christianity belongs to a remote age. Relate the study to modern literature, current philosophical trends, social problems, etc., but do not get off on tangents.

4/*The language used must communicate biblical concepts*

accurately. Listen to what *you* are saying. Watch for facial reactions or body postures that indicate you are not getting through. Avoid evangelical jargon. Explain theological language and figures of speech in a simple way.

5/*Avoid dogmatism*. Strong convictions have more effect when expressed quietly and with good reasons. Preface potentially dogmatic statements with reference to the passage, for example, "It seems to me from v. 10 and v.12 that . . ." Also, a firm comment made casually or even humorously can be very disarming.

6/*Avoid cross-references unless necessary*. Skipping all over the Bible may impress some friends with our knowledge, but it may also confuse others. Or, worse, it may discourage them. They may think a qualification for being a Christian is a high Bible I. Q.

7/*Stick to the Bible as your authority*. At the beginning of the discussion it should be agreed that the purpose is to see what the Bible says and means. Be careful also that Christians in the group do not depend on experiences or subjective opinions. Personal experience may illustrate or confirm a scriptural truth but should never upstage it.

8/*Get through the planned passage*, even if it means summarizing part of it. Getting through only a few verses each time can kill a study. It is helpful to be guided by this question: What overall impression of Jesus Christ is this study leaving with us?

9/*End the study on time*, even though discussion may (and should) continue afterwards. Converse with individuals personally on the basis of their comments and questions during the study. These conversations are often the most fruitful part of the EBS as an evangelistic effort.

10/*There should be no pressure for anyone to make a decision to become a Christian*. One should be sensitive, however, to the right time to speak to individuals about their need to give all that they know of themselves to all that they know of Jesus Christ. Surely the Holy Spirit guides here as he does during the study.

A student with a glow in his eyes once said to me after a few attempts at EBSs on his campus, "I was discouraged the first two times. Then I began to realize that leading a Bible study is partly a matter of skill and, like any skill, it can be developed with practice."

He's right. There is no "instant Bible study leadership" any more than there is "instant evangelism." But as in any of our work for the Lord, we persist by his grace, "knowing that in the Lord your labor is not in vain" (1 Cor. 15:58).

Bible study guides from InterVarsity Press

DISCUSSIONS ON THE LIFE OF JESUS CHRIST
Considers the basic message of Christianity: what Christ
is like and the implications of his claims. 402-X $1.25

BASIC CHRISTIANITY
Margaret Erb provides topical studies for non-Christians
or young Christians, with suggestions for the leader of a
group discussion. 401-1 $1.25

JESUS THE RADICAL
Ada Lum focuses on eight studies from the Gospel of
John, showing Jesus challenging the capitalists, debating
with the Establishment, crashing traditional social barriers. 316-3 95ᶜ

DISCOVERING THE GOSPEL OF MARK
Jane Hollingsworth offers directions for individual study
and for the leader of a group, plus a study chart and questions on each chapter of Mark's Gospel. 419-4 $1.25

ONE TO ONE
William M. York, Jr., presents six brief Bible studies de-
signed to help Christians acquaint their friends—on a
one-to-one basis—with the essential facts of the gospel.
438-0 $1.25